ANTIQUE
& CLASSIC WINGS

ANTIQUE & CLASSIC WINGS

David Davies

OSPREY
AEROSPACE

Published in 1992 by
Osprey Publishing Limited
59 Grosvenor Street London W1X 9DA

ISBN 1 85532 220 X

Editor Dennis Baldry
Text Mike Jerram
Page design Colin Paine
Printed in Hong Kong

Front cover A shape that simply
exudes miles per hour – Geoffrey de
Havilland's masterly D.H.88 Comet
racer. The priceless G-ACSS
Grosvenor House is featured on pages
70–76

Back cover The Gloster Gladiator
was the RAF's last biplane fighter,
and the Shuttleworth Collection's
machine is the last airworthy
example of over 750 aircraft
(including 60 Sea Gladiators for the
British Fleet Air Arm) built between
1934–1940

Title page The Shuttleworth
Collection's de Havilland D.H.60X
Hermes Moth aloft over greenest
Bedfordshire near to Old Warden
Aerodrome, its base for six decades

For a catalogue of all books published by Osprey Aerospace
please write to:

**The Marketing Department, Octopus Illustrated Books,
1st Floor, Michelin House, 81 Fulham Road, London SW3 6RB**

Corporate transport, 1934-style. 'The Sunflower Seed Co's' gorgeous four-seat Waco UKC is actually the mount of UK-based American stockbroker Paul McConnell, whose stable also includes an equally immaculate Beech D17C 'Staggerwing'

About the Author

David Davies has enjoyed a love affair with aeroplanes and photography since his early school days. His memories of weekend visits by bus or train from the West Midlands to airfields at Derby, Hawarden, Luton and Weybridge remain vivid even now. On all of these trips essential equipment, apart from notebook and pencil, was a simple camera; what better way to combine two all-consuming hobbies.

In 1959 he took an apprenticeship in professional photography, a decision which resulted in a career which continues to the present day. He recalls taking his newly acquired and much prized (but rather ancient) VN plate camera to the Paris Air Show in 1963, and having to load the glass plates into holders under bed clothes in his hotel room each night!

Towards the end of the 1960s, David Davies formed Air Portraits with fellow photographer Mike Vines, a partnership which lasted for 21 years. At the start of the 1970s, David and Mike became official photographers to the Shuttleworth Collection at Old Warden airfield in Bedfordshire, a pleasurable task which individually they still undertake today. Some of the fruits of David Davies' long association with the Shuttleworth Collection may be appreciated on the next 120 pages.

In the early 1970s David Davies also gained his Private Pilots Licence (PPL) and bought a share in a beautiful, sunburst-painted Belgian Stampe SV.4C biplane (page 69), but alas it was written-off by a colleague within a few months.

Highlight of the decade was flying with other Press photographers on the pre-Farnborough Air Show air-to-air sorties aboard a Handley-Page Hastings transport, its massive cargo door being removed so as to allow the 'snappers' to take shots of many of the Show's aircraft, which would come up to pose alongside as required. Sadly, this facility was discontinued when the venerable piston-engined Hastings was retired in the mid-1970s. David Davies has covered the Farnborough and Paris Air Shows for a major international publisher since 1978.

Recent personal milestones include the publication of his first book (the forerunner to this volume), *Antique & Classic Airplanes* in 1985, followed by *Superbase 5 Mildenhall: Multi-mission Task Force* in 1989, and *Superbase 21 Barksdale: Home of the Mighty Eighth* in 1991; all three of these Osprey books were co-authored with Mike Vines.

David Davies is a regular contributor to *Jane's All The World's Aircraft*, *PILOT Magazine*, *Aeroplane Monthly* and operates an aviation colour picture library. Readers who may wish to order copies of the photographs featured in this book are asked to contact Air Portraits, 131 Welwyndale Road, Sutton Coldfield, West Midlands B72 1AL, United Kingdom. Telephone/fax 021 373 4021.

Right Designed by Bob Hall, creator of the (in)famous Gee Bee racers, the Stinson SR Reliant first flew in 1934, but it was not until Bob Ayer's distinctive wing, evolved from that of the Stinson Model A tri-motor airliner, was added in 1936 that the classic 'Gullwing' Stinson emerged. The shapes of the rudder horn balance and engine cowlings identify N52028 as one of 500 1942-vintage military model V-77/AT-19 Reliants supplied under the Lend-Lease programme to the British Royal Navy as navigation trainers

Contents

Magnificent Flying Machines

'The control system of the Bristol biplane is simplicity itself. It can be mastered in a few minutes and it requires so little physical effort that a child can manoeuvre one of these machines in flight. There is, indeed, only one movement that calls for the slightest physical exertion, and that is the movement of the control lever away from the body to the right, but even this is felt only when there is a strong gust of wind exerting its force to tilt the machine up on one side'. So ran a 1910 sales brochure for the Bristol Boxkite, which was the first commercially produced British aeroplane, an improved version of French Farman and Voisin designs which sold for the then very considerable sum of £1100. While it did have some innovations, such as crude ailerons for lateral control, that publicity puff was at best economic with the truth. The late Neil Williams, who frequently flew the Shuttleworth Collection's replica seen here, concluded that it was 'a devil to fly', completely unstable in pitch with heavy lateral control, and could only maintain level flight at a speed of precisely 31 mph

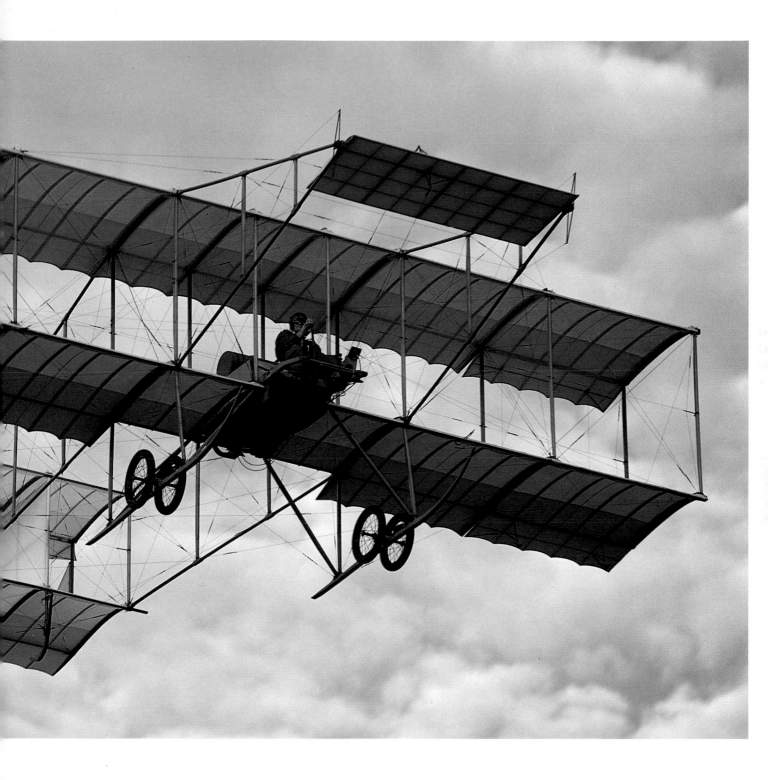

Above Boxkites were employed at the Bristol flying schools at Larkhill and Brooklands, among their students being the legendary Robert Smith-Barry, the father of the 'Gosport' pilot training system. The Boxkite was also exported to Australia, India and Russia, where eight were operated by the Imperial Russian Army. The Shuttleworth example was built in 1964 by the famous lightplane manufacturing Miles brothers for the motion picture *Those Magnificent Men in Their Flying Machines*. It differs from the original in having a modern 90 hp Lycoming flat-four engine in place of the 50 hp Gnome rotary. Whilst its aerial galleon configuration creates high drag, the Boxkite pilot enjoys an unsurpassed view of the (slowly) passing world, albeit a chilly one. When asked in 1910 what equipment might be needed by observers flying in Boxkites on army manoeuvres, the pilot replied: 'layer after layer of clothing'

Below Not since 1066 had a Frenchman's arrival on British soil been of such historic significance as Louis Blériot's landing on a clifftop near Dover on 25 July 1909 after making the first crossing of the English Channel by aeroplane. The £1000 prize awarded by newspaper baron Lord Northcliffe was no doubt welcome, but the ensuing publicity made Blériot, already wealthy from the manufacture of acetylene lamps for motor cars, a richer man still. Within two days he had received orders for more than 100 Blériot XI Monoplanes, which were widely used for training, racing and for military purposes.

Unlike the Boxkite, the Shuttleworth Trust's Blériot XI is the genuine article, built in 1909 by the pioneer himself and used by the Blériot School at Hendon near London up to 1912, when it crashed and was placed into storage under a railway arch until bought by a Bedfordshire man A E Grimmer, who rebuilt it and taught himself to fly on it before the First World War. In the old days a Blériot neophyte would learn the rudiments of control on a *Penguin* – an old timeworn machine whose wings had been clipped short so that, like its namesake, it was incapable of true flight but could manage tentative hops. Having tamed his *Penguin* the apprentice aviator would graduate to the real thing, no doubt buoyed by the knowledge that Monsieur Louis himself had less than five hours total flying time when he made his epic sea crossing

Above The Blériot XI was the first aeroplane to have a single control stick combining roll (via wing-warping) and pitch control in the same lever. This one is powered by a three-cylinder aircooled engine designed by the Italian motorcycle builder Allessandro Anzani, whose motors' reputation for dependability was matched by his own for use of the profanest language. The Blériot's engine, with its fan-shaped cylinder arrangement, puts out a nominal 24 hp on a good day, but like most of its breed is prone to plug fouling and overheating. When Louis Blériot crossed the Channel in 37 minutes his motor was probably having the longest uninterrupted run of its life, and then only kept him from a ducking in the water when a shower of rain provided some timely supplemental cooling. On later Blériots powered by Gnome rotary engines you might with luck go 12 hours or more between major overhauls. The cockpit has just the one instrument – a 'pulsometer' pressure gauge for the globular brass oil tank which must be pressurised by hand pump to maintain around two pounds per square inch pressure for the total loss oil system. Well, not *quite* total loss, since that big propeller does a fine job of sending an aerosol spray mix of castor oil and exhaust fumes back over the unprotected pilot. In the pioneering days before bottle-and-throttle rules a slug of cognac or whisky before flying was the recommended cure for the worst effects of a castor oil bath

Below and overleaf A year younger than the Blériot and also originating from France is the Deperdussin Type B 'Popular' or 'School Type', another Shuttleworth Collection treasure rebuilt by Mr Grimmer then stored before the First World War and donated to Richard Shuttleworth in 1935. The 'Dep' was designed by Louis Béchereau for Belgian silk merchant Armand Deperdussin, founder of Société Pour les Appareils Deperdussin (SPAD), whose fighters became famous during World War I, and was a predecessor of the type that won the Gordon Bennett Cup in 1913 and became the first aeroplane to exceed 200 kilometres per hour. Powered by an improved Y-shaped Anzani of 35 hp, the 'Dep' is flown with the aid of a large five-spoked control wheel that looks as if it would be more at home on the bridge of a ship; it turns to warp the wings and moves fore and aft to work the elevators. Like the Blériot it has just a single instrument, in this case a fuel quantity gauge.

The Deperdussin and the Blériot are believed to be the oldest *original* aeroplanes still flying anywhere in the world, though in deference to the 80-year-old veterans' fragility and value their flying these days is confined to straight hops within the airfield's boundary on the calmest of summer evenings

Above 'As soon as I started a turn, the low centre of gravity took charge and I got a terrific wobble, came down in a nose-dive from the great height of two feet, crashed the machine and landed on my head in the sand. However, this did not dim my faith in aeroplanes.' So wrote the British pioneer aviator Robert Blackburn after his first attempt at flight in 1910, and indeed, faith undimmed, he proceeded to develop a series of innovative monoplanes of exceptionally clean design of which the Shuttleworth Collection's 1912 Blackburn Monoplane is the sole survivor. Note Blackburn's distinctive triangular fuselage cross-section and tail surfaces, and the half-cowled 50 hp Gnome rotary engine. Blackburn devised and patented an all-in-one control system or 'triple steering column' consisting of a motor car steering wheel which worked wing-warping, elevators and rudder. This machine has rudder pedals for yaw control, retaining the steering wheel for roll and pitch control, the latter working in what now seems an unnatural sense but is actually quite logical – the wheel/column is raised to lower the nose, pushed down into the pilot's lap to raise it

Below This machine was the seventh built by Robert Blackburn and was constructed for Cyril Foggin, who learned to fly at the Blackburn School at Hendon. It was discovered, mostly hidden in a haystack, in 1937 and is the oldest original British aeroplane still flying. A strong performer still, with a maximum speed of 60 mph, it has enough climb performance on the 50 hp Gnome to essay a modest circuit of the environs of its base at Old Warden Aerodrome, a sight to be savoured by even the most jaded of aeronautical palates

Right and following pages Alliott Verdon-Roe made the first powered flight by an Englishman on 8 June 1908, though his achievement was never officially recognised. He subsequently built his Bulls-Eye Avroplane which earned its place in history as the first British-designed and -built machine to fly, on 23 July 1909. It was a triplane, and Roe subsequently built three more machines of this configuration, culminating in the 1910 Avro Mark IV. The original was powered by a 35 hp Green water-cooled engine. This replica, built by the Hampshire Aeroplane Club for *Those Magnificent Men* in which it was the mount of the dastardly 'Sir Percy' played by Terry Thomas, enjoys three times the power with its 105 hp D.H. Cirrus Hermes II, and is a fine flier, acknowledged as the best handling of all the replicas created for that landmark film. The replica builders chose not to add ailerons, retaining Roe's roll-control system which warps the outer sections of the two uppermost wings. It is barely adequate. The late Neil Williams, one of many skilled test pilots who have delighted in flying the Avro, noted that an incipient wing-drop would require the pilot to wind the wheel with the energy of a London bus driver while the Triplane gave the impression of being 'about to turn turtle, like a small yacht in a gale'. Note the fuel tank beneath centre of upper wing, and the lower wing mounted below the fuselage so that it generates lift throughout its span

Knights of the Air

When it first entered service with No 56 Sqn, Royal Flying Corps in April 1917 the Royal Aircraft Factory S.E.5 was rated 'a dud' by pilots accustomed to lightweight, nimble rotary-engined types such as the Sopwith Pup and French Nieuport 17. But the S.E.5 and its successor the S.E.5A, which was powered by 200 hp geared Hispano-Suiza (Hisso) or direct-drive Wolseley Viper V-8 engines, quickly developed into a formidable gun platform. Albert Ball, VC, scored 13 of his 44 victories on one during a 12-day period in the spring of 1917, while Major James McCudden claimed 51 of his 57 'kills' in an S.E., and himself died in one when he crashed making a fatal turn back to the airfield after his S.E.5A's engine failed on take-off

Above More than 5000 S.E.5s and S.E.5As were built, serving with 21 RFC squadrons, one Australian squadron and several training units. The Shuttleworth Collection's S.E.5A was one of a fleet used in the 1920s by the celebrated Major J C Savage for aerial advertising – 'skywriting'. Discovered in 1955 hanging engineless from the roof of a shed at the Armstrong Whitworth factory near Coventry, it was rebuilt by apprentices and staff at its birthplace, now RAE Farnborough, and flew again on 4 August 1959 in the hands of Shuttleworth Trustee the late Air Commodore Allen H Wheeler. At that time it was powered by a Hispano-Suiza, since replaced by a Viper

Below Mount of aces. The S.E.5A's armament comprised a fuselage-mounted Vickers machine gun – one of the first to employ the Constantinesco interrupter mechanism for firing between the revolving blades of propeller – and a Lewis gun mounted on a Foster rack atop the wing centre-section and fired via a Bowden cable leading into the cockpit. The Vickers was prone to jamming and synchronisation problems. Ball and other skilled exponents of the type favoured the Lewis, though reloading (note drum-like ammunition magazine) was tricky whilst flying in combat

Below Contrary to popular supposition, rotary engines are not rattling, vibrating devices, but are of necessity finely balanced to run turbine-smooth. Here the 110 hp Le Rhône engine of the Shuttleworth Avro 504K gets up to speed

Above Although it entered RFC service as a fighting aeroplane (in November 1914 four of them made history by carrying out the first pre-planned aerial bombing raid in history when they attacked the Zeppelin works at Friedrichshafen on Lake Constance), the Avro 504 achieved greatest fame as a trainer. Designer Alliott Verdon Roe thought he might win orders for six aircraft when first he submitted the 504 to the British War Office; by Armistice Day 1918 no fewer than 8340 had been built, and when production of Avro 504 sub-variants finally ceased in 1933 more than 10,000 had been produced. Most numerous was the Avro 504K, powered by 100 hp Gnome Monosoupape and Le Rhône or 130 hp Clerget engines. In peacetime surplus Avros were quickly converted to three- or even five-seat joyriding aeroplanes by touring flying circus operators. This example was built as a 504K, converted with Armstrong Siddeley Lynx engine to Avro 504N for the Royal Air Force, and subsequently 'deconverted' back to original 'K configuration by apprentices of the Avro Company. Note distinctive central landing skid to prevent nose-overs, and gravity-feed fuel tank atop the upper wing, pressurised by the small airflow-driven propeller just visible on the starboard cabane strut

Officially known as the Sopwith Scout, Tommy (later Sir Thomas) Sopwith's biplane fighter bore such a striking resemblance to the larger 1½ Strutter that it quickly gained the nickname Pup, which stayed with the machine forever thereafter. First flown in February 1916, the Pup was initially ordered for the Royal Naval Air Service and made the world's first landing on the deck of a ship under way when Squadron Leader E H Dunning set his Pup down on HMS *Furious* on 2 August 1917, only to die a few days later when his aeroplane was blown overboard before the deck crew could 'arrest' it. When the Pup entered combat in France with No 8 Sqn, RNAS, it accounted for 14 enemy aircraft destroyed and 13 damaged in its first three months of service and dominated the skies over the Western Front for much of 1917. The Shuttleworth Pup was the last of ten converted on the production line in peacetime 1918 to two-seat configuration as appropriately-named civilian Doves. Converted to single-seat scout configuration, it wears the serial number of the Pup prototype. Note leather padded windscreen set into the butt of its Vickers machine gun in the taxiing view

Though low-powered with its 80 hp Le Rhône rotary engine, the Pup weighed just 790 lbs empty, so its high power/weight ratio and generous wing area provided an excellent sustained climb rate, nimble handling and high manoeuvrability even at altitudes above 10,000 feet, while its maximum speed of 111 mph was faster than any other contemporary aeroplane using the same powerplant. Despite the lack of firepower afforded by its single fixed-mount synchronised Vickers 0.303 machine gun, the little Pup's handling made it a favourite from Sopwith's 'Zoo that Flew': James McCudden, VC, declared that it could 'outmanoeuvre any (German) Albatros no matter how good the pilot was, and when it came to manoeuvring, the Sopwith could turn twice to the Albatros's once'

A brace of Pups. The sight of one genuine original Sopwith Pup aloft is rare enough, but two . . .! On patrol over Old Warden Aerodrome in the summer of 1974 are the Shuttleworth Trust's G-EBKY/N5180 (nearest camera with red/white wheel discs) in the hands of Squadron Leader 'Dickie' Martin, and Desmond St Cyrien's G-APUP/N5182 flown by the late Neil Williams. N5180 is still very active, N5182 firmly grounded in the Royal Air Force Museum at Hendon

Designed by Herbert Smith, creator of the later Camel which was to eclipse it in service, the Sopwith Triplane was an attempt to create an even more manoeuvrable scout than the Pup. The prototype was first flown by Harry Hawker on 28 May 1916, and the Triplane entered service with the Royal Naval Air Service in February 1917. Between May and July 1917 five pilots of B Flight, No 10 Sqn RNAS destroyed 87 enemy aircraft, with flight leader F/Sub-Lieutenant Raymond Collishaw personally accounting for 16 in 27 days. The Triplane's career was glorious, though brief, and by late 1917 it had disappeared from the Western Front, replaced by the Sopwith Camel. The Triplane pictured here is a full-scale authentic replica. Built for Christies director and historic aircraft collector The Honourable Patrick Lindsay, it is now part of the Weeks Air Museum Collection in Florida

Though designed (by Gustave Delage) and built in France, the elegant though undistinguished Nieuport 28.C1's history is inextricably linked with the American Expeditionary force, which operated 297 of them during the final months of the First World War. Powered by a 160 hp Gnome Monosoupape 9N nine-cylinder rotary engine, it was the first design from the Nieuport stable to abandon the sesquiplane wing configuration in favour of a two-spar lower wing with chord almost equal to that of the upper surface. The example seen here is owned by the Historic Aviation Collection of Jersey, and was formerly part of the Tallmantz Movieland of the Air Museum in California, where it may have been one of several Nieuport 28.C1s to star in the classic movies *The Dawn Patrol* and *Hell's Angels*. Restored from a 'basket case' by Skysport Engineering in England, it wears the colourful kicking mule insignia of the AEF's 95th Aero Squadron

Two seaters from opposing sides in the Great War, now united in the Shuttleworth Collection.

Above After an inauspicious service entry by an earlier variant, the Bristol F.2B, with water-cooled 275 hp Rolls-Royce Falcon III V-12 engine, fixed forward-firing Vickers gun and one or two Scarff-ring-mounted Lewis guns, became the Allies' most effective fighting aeroplane of the First World War, and a mainstay of the Royal Air Force in peacetime. 4469 'Brisfits' or 'Biffs' were built. This is currently the only airworthy example. Note how designer Frank Barnwell mounted the aircraft's fuselage mid-way between the sets of wings, providing pilot and observer/gunner with a view over the top of the upper surface.

Below The 1917 LVG C.VI was a German reconnaissance and artillery observation platform, of which some 1100 examples were built by the Berlin-based *Luft-Verkehrs-Gesellschaft* (Air Transport Company). Powered by a 230 hp Benz BzIV engine and armed with a fixed Spandau machine gun offset to the starboard side of the cockpit and a flexible-mount Parabellum for the observer, it was a strong and steady, if cumbersome, machine which performed well enough in its intended roles, but proved an easy target for opposing scouts. The exposed slow-revving six cylinder Benz engine with its distinctive 'rhino horn' vertical exhaust stack, observer's position, five-colour lozenge pattern upper surface fabric and architypal German shape tail unit configuration are well illustrated in this view. Forced down by two No 74 Sqn S.E.5As on 2 August 1918, the LVG C.VI was shipped to Britain as war booty and briefly tested against contemporary British aircraft (including the Bristol Fighter) before many years of storage, interrupted by a flying appearance at the 1937 Hendon Air Display. It was fully (and very faithfully) restored by Shuttleworth Collection staff and members of the Shuttleworth Veteran Aeroplane Society in the 1970s and is the only genuine German two-seater from the First World War still flying

Moth Magic

'My enthusiasm for natural history led me to seek the solution in entymology', said Sir Geoffrey de Havilland of his search in 1925 for a suitable name for his D.H.60 'Aeroplane for All'. He chose Moth, which was destined to become not only the family title of a whole range of pre-war designs from the de Havilland stable, but in popular parlance also a generic term for *any* British light aeroplane of the era.

G-EBWD seen here on take-off from Old Warden Aerodrome was built in 1928 as a D.H.60X Cirrus Moth, powered by a 65 hp D.H. Cirrus I four-cylinder engine (the X in the designation signified a change to a split-axle type undercarriage, visible in the rear view, which was more forgiving of 'firm' landings than the earlier straight-axle type). Richard Shuttleworth bought it in 1932 for £300 and made his first solo flight in the aeroplane at Brooklands. Re-engined the following year with a 105 hp Hermes II, G-EBWD has been based at Shuttleworth's home at Old Warden, Bedfordshire since its acquisition – the longest that an airworthy aeroplane has remained at the same aerodrome continuously in aviation history – and celebrated its Diamond Jubilee at the airfield on 14 February 1992

While not strictly speaking a Moth at all, D.H.51 G-EBIR bears an unmistakable family likeness, though it predated the D.H.60 by a year. Designed as a tourer, with single-seat pilot's cockpit to rear and two tandem-seated passengers in front, the D.H.51 made its first flight in the hands of Geoffrey de Havilland on 1 July 1924. Though docile to handle and well-suited to its purpose, it proved too expensive for most private owners, and only three were built. G-EBIR was the third and last, and was shipped to owner John Carberry in Kenya in September 1925 where it became VP-KAA *Miss Kenya*, the first aeroplane of Kenyan registry. In 1965 the uniquely surviving example was airfreighted from Nairobi to London for restoration by its manufacturer, then part of the Hawker Siddeley Aviation Group, and donated in 1973 to the Shuttleworth Trust. The 120 hp Airdisco-powered *Miss Kenya* is presently the oldest de Havilland design flying anywhere in the world, though it will give up that title to its Shuttleworth companion the D.H.53 Humming Bird when plans to return that aircraft to airworthiness come to fruition during 1992

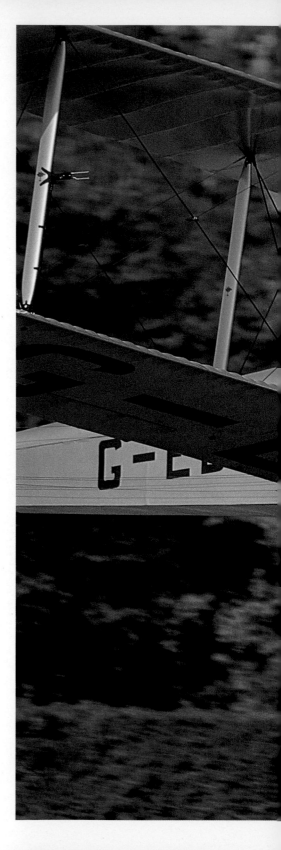

Above D.H.60G Gipsy Moth cockpits. Note original instrumentation, including large turn-and-slip indicator bottom left in rear cockpit, and long exhaust pipe running alongside the cockpit to port, providing very welcome warming air but a painful reminder of its presence to any unwary passenger trailing an ungloved hand outside

Below and following pages G-EBLV is the earliest surviving example of the D.H.60 Moth, known among its many admirers in the D.H. Moth Club as 'Mother Moth'. Also the most original survivor of the species, it is powered by the 60 hp ADC Cirrus I four-cylinder engine which de Havilland's chief engineer Major Frank Halford developed from one half of a war-surplus 120 hp Airdisco-Renault V-8. G-EBLV was the eighth Moth built, and was delivered new in July 1925 to the Lancashire Aero Club at Woodford Aerodrome by the famous pioneer aviator Alan Cobham. Back then, Moths sold for £885, the price quickly dropping as the economies of large-scale production took hold to £730 including tool kit, covers for engine, cockpits and propeller and a choice of colour scheme. De Havilland set up a worldwide network of sales and service stations and ran vigorous publicity campaigns which included putting a Moth

in the window of a large department store in London's Oxford Street. Flying instruction was often included in the purchase price. At D.H.'s home airfield at Stag Lane individual lock-up 'Moth garages' were available at a rent of one pound per week in which to store your Moth, wings folded, while company ground staff were on hand to service, clean and prepare it for flight, though the manufacturer made a point of assuring would-be owners that their Moth 'could be kept in perfect order by anybody with only ordinary knowledge of motor cars' and that its Cirrus engine was 'as straightforward and reliable as a motorcycle engine … runs on commercial brands of petrol and oil obtainable from any wayside garage'. The sight of a Moth filling up at a roadside petrol station was not uncommon. You won't find G-EBLV by any roadside, though. Today she is owned, cherished and maintained in pristine airworthy order by British Aerospace, successor to de Havilland, and based not far from her Stag Lane birthplace at the company airfield at Hatfield

Mating the 85 hp D.H. Gipsy engine with the Moth airframe created the classic, enduring Gipsy Moth which first appeared during 1928 and quickly caught public attention when three entered that year's King's Cup Air Race and W L Hope won the coveted trophy at 105 mph. Captain Geoffrey de Havilland later set an altitude record of 19,980 feet in his own Gipsy Moth, while test pilot Hubert Board stayed aloft over Stag lane for 24 hours in a modified Gipsy Moth with additional fuel tanks. The Gipsy engine was a masterpiece – light, powerful and totally reliable, so much so that an engine taken straight from the production line was sealed, installed in a Gipsy Moth airframe and flown for 600 hours over a nine-month period without maintenance save for routine greasing and topping-up of oil. It covered 51,000 miles for a total cost in overhaul and replacement parts of just over £7. This Gipsy Moth, sadly wrecked in 1972 but likely to reappear one day, is a de luxe variant (note streamlined headrest fairing) whose original purchase price would have included a set of wheel chocks, tailskid trolley and a shooting stick

Though it came close to being 'everyman's aeroplane', the Gipsy Moth did not suit the Royal Air Force, its front cockpit arrangement beneath centre-section fuel tank and amid cabane struts proving too difficult for a pilot encumbered with parachute and bulky military flying clothing to exit in a hurry. Designer Arthur Hagg moved the cabane struts forward to clear the front cockpit, maintained aerodynamic equilibrium by sweeping the wings back through the simple expedient of shortening the rear spars, installed a new 120 hp Gipsy III inverted inline engine and *voila!* – thus in 1931 was created the D.H.82 Tiger Moth, the best known Moth of all. The archetypal 130 hp Gipsy Major-powered D.H.82A Tiger Moth Mk II illustrated here appeared in 1934

Above and preceding pages During the Second World War Tiger Moth Mk II trainers for the Royal Air Force were mass-produced on production lines at the D.H. factory at Hatfield and by the Morris Motor Works near Oxford, while others were manufactured by de Havilland subsidiaries in Australia, Canada (where a special 'Canadianised' D.H.82C version was developed) and New Zealand, and under licence by companies in Norway, Portugal and Sweden. Total production numbers are the subject of vigorous debate among historians and afficionados, but 9231 is the most oft-quoted figure. This one, restored in authentic World War 2 training colours of Dark/Light Earth and Dark/Light Green camouflage on top surfaces (dark colours on top wing, light on the lower surface) and Trainer Yellow undersurfaces, belongs to the Shuttleworth Collection. The diamond-shaped marking on the rear turtledeck is a gas detection patch, designed to change colour in the event of the gas attacks which were a much-feared though fortunately never realised threat in the early wartime years

Left Who knows how many tens or even hundreds of thousands of neophyte fliers endured hours of ham-fisted frustration during their basic training in a cockpit such as this before getting to grips with the Tiger Moth? Trickier to fly accurately than some of its contemporaries, with a knack of exaggerating every little shortcoming in handling technique (though never to the point of becoming dangerous), the Tiger Moth made an excellent trainer, and was popular with instructors, apart from its Gosport speaking tube inter-cockpit communication system, whose black rubber mouthpiece left its Minstrel-like mark long after the day's work had ended and did little to enhance instructor/pupil communication. Note fold-down doors on both sides of the cockpit, characteristic Sutton seat harness, large centrally-mounted compass, and automatic-slat locking lever/quadrant (right side below instrument panel) in this cockpit view. A Tiger's open cockpit is a draughty place, making a thick flying jacket desirable even on a balmy summer's day

Above At war's end surplus Tiger Moths were disposed of for as little as £25 apiece, often bought for the value of the fuel remaining in their tanks, then scrapped. The survivors soldiered on as the mainstay of civilian flying clubs until newer purpose-built types came on the scene. Today they are treasured antiques, changing hands for prices one thousand-fold or more those paid for post-war give-aways, their numbers actually increasing as 'new' aircraft emerge from protracted rebuilds. The appropriately Moth-like example in the foreground here is D.H. Moth Club and Diamond Nine Formation Team's stalwart Peter Jackson's 'hi-tech' Tiger, with many fairings and non-structural items constructed of advanced composite materials

Right and below A Tiger Moth made for four. In the mid-1950s, prompted by the lack of suitable light touring aeroplanes in Britain, the Wiltshire Aeroplane Club at Thruxton Aerodrome developed a four-seat version of the ubiquitous Tiger Moth in which its steel-tube forward fuselage frame was split vertically, widened in the cockpit area from 24 to 37 inches to accommodate two staggered pairs of seats under an enclosed canopy, and mated to a standard rear fuselage and tail section. Centre-section fuel tank and wheel track were also widened, and the engine firewall and mountings moved forward to maintain centre of gravity. The resultant Thruxton Jackarro (derived from an Australian term for 'Jack of all trades') made its first flight on 2 March 1957. Eighteen Tiger Moths metamorphisised into Jackaroos between 1957–59, the last, G-APAM, becoming solo record-breaking aviatrix Sheila Scott's *Myth*. Ironically most surviving Jackaroos, including *Myth*, have since reverted back to standard (and more valuable) Tiger configuration

Overleaf Spot the interloper. Six Tigers and, in the box position, a Hornet Moth 'cabin job'

These pages and overleaf The D.H.87 appeared in 1934 as a potential Gipsy Moth replacement. Featuring a two-seat side-by-side enclosed cabin with centrally-mounted Y-shaped dual control column enabling it to be flown from either seat, it had mixed welded steel tube and wooden fuselage and wood-and-fabric wings which folded alongside for easy storage. The Hornet Moth entered production as the D.H.87A in August 1935. This initial model had elegant, sharply-tapered wings which quickly revealed a tendency to tip stall and drop a wing sharply at low airspeed – an undesirable trait for an aeroplane intended for the private owner market – and was succeeded by the D.H.87B with the less aesthetically pleasing but aerodynamically superior square-tipped wings shown here. Most earlier models were also retrofitted

A total of 165 Hornet Moths had been built by the time production ended in May 1938, half of them for export. With room for two adults, two large suitcases, 35 gallons of fuel sufficient for a range of 600 miles, and a cruising speed of 111 mph on its 130 bp D.H. Gipsy Major I engine, the Hornet Moth proved a popular tourer both pre- and post-war, the handful of surviving examples much prized by their owners. The wide undercarriage leg fairings visible in these pictures swivel through ninety degrees to act as airbrakes, a novelty first introduced on the D.H.80 Puss Moth high-wing monoplane

The D.H.94 Moth Minor was first flown by Geoffrey de Havilland on 22 June 1937 and was intended as a modern low-wing successor to the highly successful but obsolescent Moth. Powered by a specially-designed 90 hp D.H. Gipsy Minor engine, it combined the proven plywood-skinned box-style fuselage structure of the original D.H.60 with a high-aspect ratio plywood-skinned wing which drew on lessons learned from design of the D.H.88 Comet racer (see following chapter) and D.H.91 Albatross four-engined airliner. Production got under way at Hatfield during 1939 and reached some 100 aircraft before being curtailed in September of that year when war was declared and space at the factory was needed for the war effort. All Moth Minor drawings, jigs, tools and unfinished airframes were shipped to de Havilland Aircraft Pty Ltd in Australia, where final assembly and limited new production took place, including a batch of at least 40 for the Royal Australian Air Force for interim use as trainers pending quantity production of Tiger Moths. Though most Moth Minors had tandem open cockpits, a number were completed as cabin models, and others, like G-AFNG illustrated, were converted to coupé tops after surviving the war

Speed Seekers

The ultimate de Havilland? It is hard to believe that the stunningly sleek D.H.88 Comet was a contemporary of the Moths and Tiger Moths in the preceding chapter, or that this quintessentially beautiful machine is nearly 60 years old. Its design was inspired by Australian philanthropist Sir MacPherson Robertson's offer of £15,000 prize money for an air race from England to Australia in 1934 to commemorate the centenary of the founding of the State of Victoria. Most would-be competitors were forced to adapt existing designs for the 12,300 mile flight. De Havilland, with tremendous foresight, offered to produce a specialised machine for the nominal sum of £5500 each, and received orders straight from the drawing board for three Comets, one each for A O Edwards, managing director of London's Grosvenor House Hotel; aviators Jim and Amy Mollison; and racing driver Bernard Rubin

The Comet was designed and built in just nine months, a remarkable achievement because it represented a quantum leap in aircraft design and incorporated a wealth of innovation. To achieve the high speed and long range essential for the MacRobertson Race clean aerodynamic lines, minimal frontal area and a high standard of surface smoothness were essential – features which did not sit well with a need for good short field performance at some of the remote en route stops which would be required for refuelling. Thus the Comet incorporated a unique stressed-skin wooden construction which drew heavily on boatbuilding techniques, skinning being built up with diagonally-laid spruce strips.

The six-cylinder 230 hp D.H. Gipsy Six R high-compression engines were clothed in exceptionally sleek nacelles which also housed the retractable main undercarriage, and were equipped with two-position Ratier propellers which were set (with the aid of a bicycle pump!) to fine pitch for take-off and automatically returned to coarse pitch for cruising when the aircraft exceeded 140 mph. The slim fuselage incorporated a tandem two-seat cockpit and also housed all fuel, in three tanks situated ahead of the crew which gave a maximum range of 2925 miles. The first of the three Comets ordered flew from Hatfield on 8 September 1934, just six weeks before the start of the race

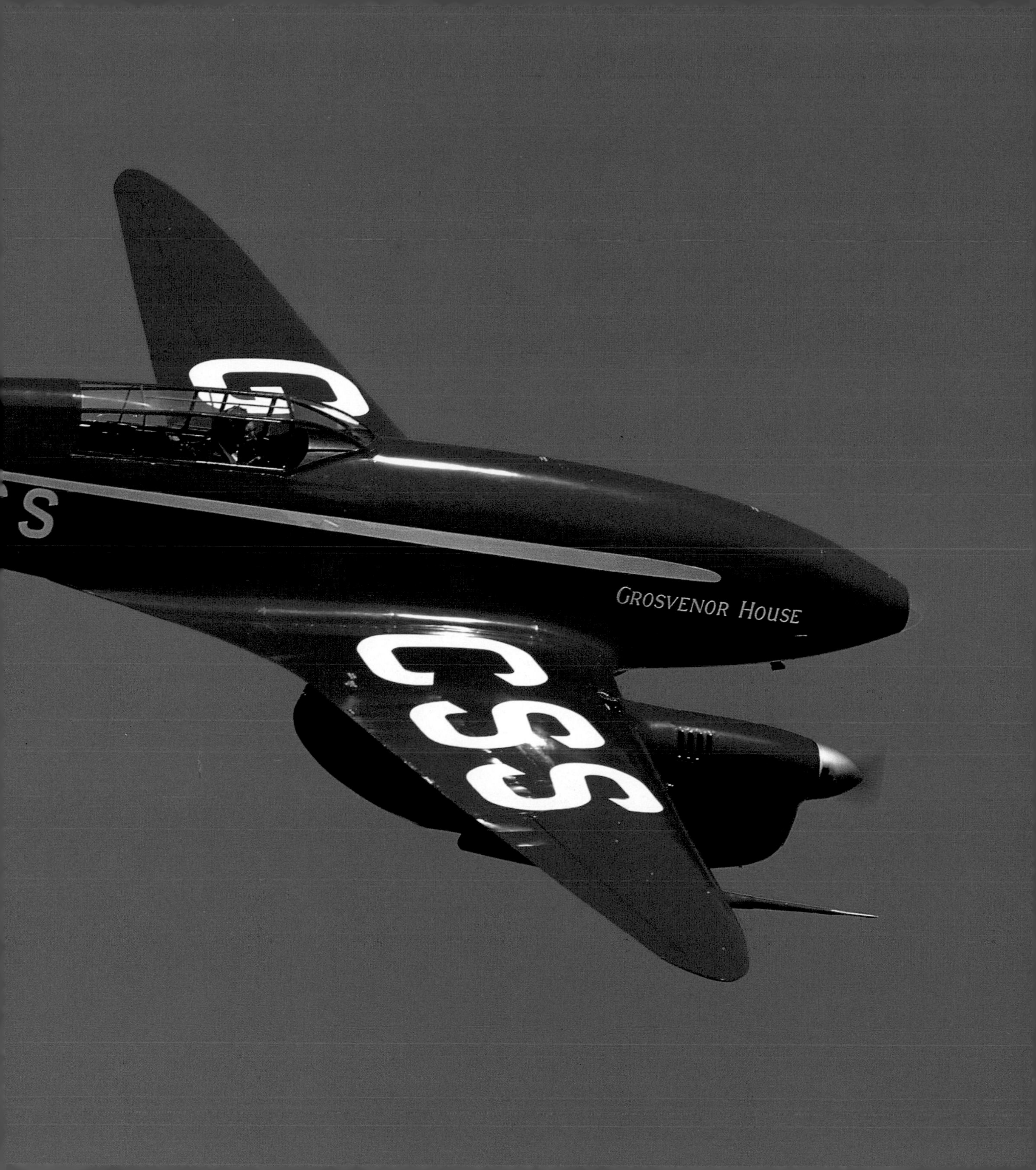
GROSVENOR HOUSE
CSS

But for the modern Cessnas in the background this could be the scene at RAF Mildenhall, Suffolk on the eve of the start of the MacRobertson Race on 20 October 1934. Three Comets were on the start line at dawn that day: the Mollisons' black-and-gold G-ACSP *Black Magic*, Rubin's green and unnamed G-ACSR flown by Owen Cathcart-Jones and Ken Waller, and Edwards' appropriately named G-ACSS *Grosvenor House*, piloted by Charles Scott and Tom Campbell-Black. The Mollisons and Scott/Campbell-Black flew non-stop to Baghdad, while Cathcart-Jones and Waller had to make an unscheduled stop in Persia because of compass problems and weather. Fortunes changed though, and engine trouble forced *Black Magic* to retire to Allahabad, while *Grosvenor House* streaked on, its crew enduring technical, weather and fatigue problems, to arrive first at Melbourne in an elapsed time of 70 hours 54 minutes and 18 seconds. The Comet had won both the speed and handicap events, though rules prevented acceptance of both so Scott and Campbell Black opted for the speed award. Cathcart-Jones and Waller's Comet placed fourth, and immediately made the return trip to England carrying newsreel film and press photographs of their rivals' triumph! And these photographs? Taken at Hatfield, birthplace of the Comet, as *Grosvenor House* was being prepared in May 1987 for its first flight in 49 years after one of the most complex and challenging historic aircraft restorations ever undertaken

Two further Comets were built after the MacRobertson Race, but only G-ACSS has survived. Briefly used by the Royal Air Force for trials during which it was damaged, it was rebuilt by Essex Aero Ltd's gifted engineer Jack Cross, and carrying the names *The Orphan* and later *The Burberry*, it made several long-distance flights in 1937/38 before being placed into open storage at Gravesend Aerodrome throughout the Second World War. Superficially restored for exhibition at the Festival of Britain in 1951, the famous racer again fell into decline while stored at the de Havilland engine factory at Leavesden, but was donated to the Shuttleworth Collection for static display in 1965. Restoration to airworthiness began in 1976, launched by grants from The Transport Trust and Hawker Siddeley Aviation. More than 50 aviation industry companies subsequently became involved in the work, which was undertaken at Old Warden, the Royal Aircraft Establishment at Farnborough, and finally at the British Aerospace plant at Hatfield, where *Grosvenor House* returned to the air on 17 May 1987 and is currently based, the short grass runways at the Shuttleworth Collection's airfield being unsuitable for safe operation of the high-performance, tricky-handling thoroughbred

Above and overleaf Not a racing aeroplane (though examples were entered in post-war Bendix Trophy transcontinental speed dashes in the USA), the D.H.98 Mosquito earns its place here as a progeny of the D.H.88 Comet racer, whose success inspired Geoffrey de Havilland to create a light, fast, all-wood, twin-engined bomber powered by two Rolls-Royce Merlins that would fly faster than most contemporary interceptors and could thus be unarmed, using its superior speed for defence. Undeterred by official myopia (the Air Ministry rejected his proposal out of hand), de Havilland undertook the 'bomber-with-fighter-speed' project as a private venture, building the prototype in total secrecy, and was ultimately rewarded with an initial order for fifty examples of the as yet unflown Mosquito in March 1940. Like its racing forerunner, the 'Wooden Wonder' embodied some novel design features, particularly its fuselage structure which was formed from laminations of birch ply with an

infilling of balsa wood and made in two halves, split vertically like a plastic model kit so that all equipment, pipework, electrical wiring and control runs could be installed before the halves were joined.

So versatile did the Mosquito prove to be that it was adapted to multitudinous roles, including fighter-bomber, night intruder, pathfinder, photo-reconnaissance aircraft, anti-shipping strike, torpedo bomber, high-speed courier, multi-engine trainer, and target tug. The RAF flew its last operational Mossie sorties – photo recce flights over Malaya – in December 1955. A total of 7781 Mosquitos were built by the de Havilland factories in Britain, Australia and Canada, and by Standard Motors, Percival Aircraft and Airspeed Aviation. Only two 'Mossies' survive in airworthy condition, one in Britain, the other in Florida. Seen here is British Aerospace's RR299. Built in 1945 as a dual-control Mosquito T Mk 3 trainer, it retired from active service in March 1963, later starred in the movies *633 Squadron* and *Mosquito Squadron* and is maintained in pristine condition by staff at BAe's factory at Hawarden, near Chester, one of the wartime production sites

Below and overleaf Pedigree Percival. Captain Edgar Percival designed and built the prototype E.1 Mew Gull in a few months in early 1934 as his personal single-seat fast tourer. Developed as the E.2 of 1935, which was essentially an entirely new aeroplane, the Mew Gull was destined to become famous as a racer and record breaker. Four E.2s and the Captain's own personal E.3H were built, the best known being G-AEXF which has had a long and illustrious, if occasionally chequered, career.

Built as one of a batch of three 205 hp D.H. Gipsy Six Series II-engined Mew Gulls entered for the £10,000 prize 1936 Schlesinger Air Race from Portsmouth, England to Johannesburg, South Africa, this aircraft was registered ZS-AHM and named *The Golden City/Die Goudstad* and flown by veteran South African pilot Major Alastair Miller, who was forced to retire from the race at Belgrade because of fuel feed problems. Subsequently re-engined with a 200 hp Gipsy Six, the Mew Gull was acquired by British pilot Alex Henshaw in exchange for a Leopard Moth. With the assistance of Jack Cross of Essex Aero Ltd at Gravesend Aerodrome, Henshaw set about preparing the aircraft for the 1938 air racing season, installing a 230 hp Gipsy Six R engine (taken from the D.H.88 Comet G-ACSS seen earlier in this chapter) with Ratier variable-pitch propeller and making many external changes to the aircraft including a low-profile cockpit canopy and close-fitting wheel spats. On its first competitive outing G-AEXF took second place in a Hatfield–Isle of Man race at the fastest speed of 247 mph with power in reserve, and subsequently took the coveted King's Cup at the then fastest ever speed of 236.5 mph. Turning their attention to the England-South Africa-England record, Henshaw and Cross replaced the temperamental 'R' engine with a less powerful but more reliable Gipsy Six II and more than doubled the aircraft's fuel capacity to 87 gallons. On 5 February 1939 Henshaw set off from Gravesend bound for Cape Town, returning in an elapsed time of four days, ten hours and 20 minutes after a meteoric out-and-back trip that established a record which has never been broken.

G-AEXF was sold in France just before the outbreak of the Second World War and remained there, hidden from the occupying Nazis, throughout the conflict. Returned to England in 1950, damaged, totally rebuilt, and progressively modified with a succession of ever larger and more unsightly canopies to improve the pilot's view, it was raced for several years in the mid-1950s, once again gaining victory in the King's Cup Race of 1955. Damaged once more in 1965 the historic racer fell into the hands of a so-called 'preservation' group who sawed its wings off to get it onto a truck, but fortunately the wreck was bought (for just £350) in 1972 by Tom Storey and Martin Barraclough, who totally rebuilt the Mew Gull to original 1936 configuration. It flew again in June 1978, watched by Alex Henshaw and Jack Cross, and was reunited with its creator Edgar Percival, still wearing his omnipresent brown trilby hat which had dictated the height of the original canopy configuration, at that year's King's Cup meeting. Alas, in 1983 a pilotless light aircraft taxied into the Mew Gull, inflicting severe damage once more, and again it was rebuilt. Then, on 6 May 1985, while on an air test by prospective purchaser Desmond Penrose, G-AEXF came to grief once more when it struck a freshly dug and unmarked drainage ditch while landing on a grass runway, somersaulted, and broke in two. Penrose, seen here in 'XF's cockpit after its fourth and latest (but probably not last) major rebuild, acquired the aircraft, and with Alex Henshaw as adviser and the assistance of Skysport Engineering and staff at the Shuttleworth Collection, painstakingly restored the Mew Gull to its Cape Record configuration. Fate was not done yet. Eleven months and less than five flying hours after its post-rebuild 'first flight' the Mew's engine failed shortly after take-off from Old Warden Aerodrome. Former test pilot Penrose made a textbook forced landing in a field of standing crop, but during the roll-out barley fouled the Mew Gull's close-fitting wheel spats and once again it somersaulted, tearing off its wings and trapping the pilot for several anxious minutes as the cockpit filled with petrol fumes from leaking fuel lines. Having risen from so many calamities, who will bet that the Mew Gull will not fly again?

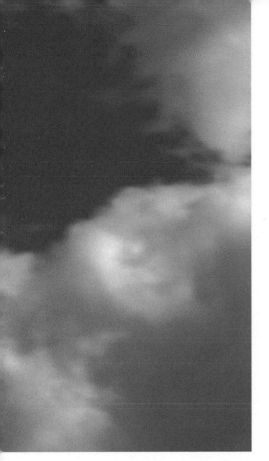

Rivals for Edgar Percivals's pre-war speedsters were the svelte single-seat racers of the Miles brothers F G and George. This is the 200 hp D.H. Gipsy Six 1F-powered M.2L Hawk Speed Six G-ADGP, one of three Speed Sixes built and the survivor of a pair constructed in 1935 for brother and sister Luis and Ruth Fontes. Raced in the thirties by the renowned long-distance flier, air racer, Miles test pilot and (prior to Alex Henshaw) holder of the England–South Africa–England record Tommy Rose, in post-war years this aircraft, fitted with a large sideways-hinged bubble canopy, was a familiar sight on the British racing scene in the hands of Ron Paine. It frequently put up the fastest time in the annual King's Cup event, but, thanks to the event's handicapping system, was never to win. After several years of obscurity in the United States during the 1980s it returned to England, where Ron Souch rebuilt the unique Hawk Speed Six to its pre-war configuration with tiny sliding 'speed' cockpit hood and black and cream colour scheme. Though owned by American Tom Buffalo, the Speed Six is on temporary loan to the Shuttleworth Collection at Old Warden and is seen here in the hands of its regular pilot and former Mew Gull co-owner Martin Barraclough

These pages Another of Edgar Percival's own designs, the all-wood three-seat Type D Gull first flew in 1932 and was raced by the Captain himself in that year's round-Britain King's Cup Air Race, averaging 142.73 mph. The ultimate D.3 or Gull Six appeared in 1935, and was substantially different from earlier models, having a 200 hp D.H. Gipsy Six engine, split trailing-edge flaps, a new more streamlined windscreen and single-strut spatted undercarriage. Of exceptionally clean design, Gulls were among the fastest private owner aeroplanes of their day, the D.3 having a top speed of 178 mph, and set many speed and distance records. Edgar Percival flew a Gull Six from Gravesend to Algeria and back in a day. Note in this view of Gull Six G-ADPR's cockpit the single front seat for the pilot, offset to the left with 'spade' type control column grip, and the large compass mounted alongside

New Zealand- born aviatrix Jean Batten bought G-ADPR new in 1935 for £1725 ('every penny I possessed', she claimed) with the intention of making a flight across the South Atlantic in it, to which end it was fitted with an 85-gallon capacity fuel tank in place of the rear passenger seats giving it a range in excess of 2000 miles. On 11 November 1935 she left Lympne in Kent bound for Brazil, which she reached after a 13 hour 15 minute transatlantic crossing, and was awarded the Britannia Trophy for her record achievement. In the two following years she made record-breaking flights from England to Australia, the first ever flight from England to her native New Zealand, and from Australia to England. G-ADPR is not part of the Shuttleworth Collection and is seen here in the hands of test pilot Angus McVitie during an air test following and extensive rebuild completed in May 1990. Later that year the famous Gull Six returned to New Zealand on temporary loan for an exhibition commemorating Jean Batten's achievements, this time making the trip rather more quickly than her 1936 record of 11 days 45 minutes by travelling in the cargo hold of a Boeing 747 freighter

Open-top Style

These pages The British company Arrow Aircraft (Leeds) Ltd built only two aeroplanes, yet remarkably one has survived in airworthy condition. The Arrow Active Mk II all-metal single-seat biplane was built in 1932 and raced in the 1932 and 1933 King's Cup events. Stored from 1935 until 1957, it became the property of the late Norman Jones, founder of the famous Tiger Club, and was rebuilt to flying condition with a 145 hp D.H. Gipsy Major IC engine replacing the original 120 hp Gipsy III. For many years the Active was raced, displayed and aerobatted by Tiger Club members, yet had only flown a total of 500 hours by 1976 when Lewis 'Benjy' Benjamin bought it, subsequently selling shares in the 'Old Girl' to a number of other Tiger Club pilots. Among them was G-ABVE's present owner Desmond Penrose, who placed second in the 1980 King's Cup with it. Beginning in 1981 Penrose has undertaken an immaculate restoration job to return the little biplane to its original 1932 specification, a task finally completed in 1989 when a zero-timed Gipsy III engine, originally fitted to the fifth production Tiger Moth, was installed in place of its more powerful successor. Like many of the unique vintage machines in this book, the Arrow Active is housed with the Shuttleworth Collection at Old Warden

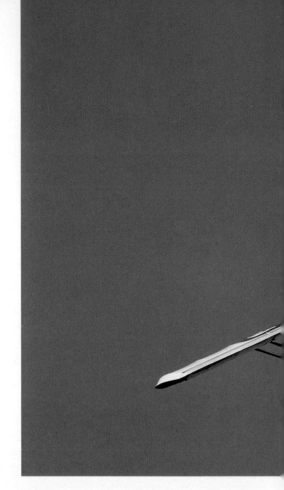

Below and right Another Old Warden resident and long-time survivor from a small production run is the Parnall Elf, three of which were built by the woodworking firm of George Parnall & Co of Yate near Bristol between 1929–32. Designed by Harold Bolas, the first Elf made its public debut at the Olympia Aero Show in London in July 1929. The Elf was a two-seater with plywood-skinned fuselage and fabric-covered folding wings which were braced, as clearly shown in the rear view, by arranging the interplane struts to form a Warren girder truss, so dispensing with the usual biplane array of flying and landing wires. G-AAIN was the second Elf built, first flown in June 1932 and sold to Lord Apsley at Badminton. After wartime storage it was acquired in non-flying condition by the Shuttleworth Collection in 1951 and restored by apprentices to fly again during 1980. It is powered by a 105 hp Hermes II four-cylinder inline engine

Left Though a tandem two-seater, G-AAIN has its front cockpit covered, and is soloed from this rear position. Note detented 'tail trimmer' to the left of the control column for adjusting tailplane incidence

Parasols up over Buckinghamshire. The Honourable Patrick Lindsay's splendid Morane-Saulnier M.S. 230 aloft from its base at Booker Aerodrome in the early 1970s. The French-built M.S. 230 was introduced in 1930 and formed the nucleus of the *Armée de l'Air*'s pre-war basic training fleet. Many survived in military service and with French flying clubs into the 1950s and beyond. The 250 hp Samson 9Ab radial-engined machine was also licence-produced in Belgium and Portugal, and spawned a variety of sub-types. In this view owner Lindsay is in the rear seat, with Manx Kelly up front, both now sadly deceased and much missed on the historic aircraft and airshow scenes

Right Self portrait. The author, suitably attired as befits an open-cockpit pilot, aloft in his sunburst-striped Stampe SV.4C over the West Midlands in 1972

Left Often erroneously referred to as 'a French Tiger Moth', the Stampe SV.4 was actually of Belgian origin, designed in 1933 by Jean Stampe and Maurice Vertongen as a two-seat open-cockpit sporting and training biplane. Although small numbers were manufactured in its homeland for the Belgian Air Force, most Stampes were built post-war by SNCA du Nord in France, which delivered some 700 D.H. Gipsy Major-powered SV.4Bs and Renault-engined SV.4Cs to the *Armée de l'Air* and *L'Aeronavalé*, and to government-sponsored civilian flying clubs in France. In the 1950s Stampes dominated European aerobatic competitions, and still make excellent basic aerobatic trainers. Of the 977 Stampes built, some 350 are thought to still exist, including 60 in Britain, half of them airworthy. This one, as its personalised registration suggests, was the property of noted British aerobaticist Richard Goode, these days to be found cavorting in the rather more capable Extra 300 and Sukhoi Su-26MX competition monoplanes

Below Bébé over the numbers. Designed by the father-in-law/son-in-law team of Edouard JOly and Jean DELmontez, the Jodel D.9 Bébé is one of the most enduring homebuilt lightplane designs, still popular with amateur aeroplane constructors more than four decades after its first flight in France on 21 January 1948. A simple all-wood airframe, usually powered by a converted Volkswagen aircooled engine (the second prototype used one of the many left behind after the war by the occupying German forces), the Bébé has been built in untold numbers worldwide and inspired a host of similarly 'bent-winged' two- and four-seat homebuilt and series production aircraft, culminating in the Robin DR400 series lightplanes which are still being manufactured at Dijon

These pages Time was when leathery-faced itinerant barnstormers would tour the USA in biplanes not so very different (though seldom as shiny and well cared for) as this lovely 1928 New Standard D-25A, landing in farm pastures to erect their bedsheet signs *FLY! - $5 - FLY!* and give folk a sight of Hometown from the air. Today the price may have gone up, but the thrill's still there. $20 gets you a smile from the attractive ground crew and a seat in the four-place open cabin ahead of the pilot, while the 220 hp Wright radial soon has you aloft, thrilled by the horizon-to-horizon view, cheeks aglow from the sheer pleasure of it (and maybe from the wind on your face). Worth every cent! But then, it always was . . .

Above The name's WACO. *Wah*-co. Not Way-co, like the Texas town, nor
Whacko, and it stands for Weaver Aircraft Company, which was set up in 1919
by Clayton Brukner and 'Sam' Junkin. Waco, which after several moves set up
permanent home in Troy, Ohio, built a large range of open-cockpit and cabin
biplanes during the 1920s and 1930s for use as trainers, business aircraft and –
particularly in South America – for military purposes. This one is a three-seat
(two in front, one behind) UPF-7, the most numerous of all Waco variants
thanks to its selection for the US Civilian Pilot Training programme
inaugurated in 1940 to boost the number of trained pilots against the threat of
war, which duly came to pass. Waco built 600 220 hp Continental radial-
engined UPF-7s, the last leaving the factory on 7 November 1942 when the
company turned its facilities over to production of troop-carrying gliders

Below *Ask any Pilot* was Waco's slogan. Unfortunately the author didn't ask this pilot what kind of Waco he was flying – an essential enquiry for all but the most dedicated student of the breed, for Waco type numbers are a confusing alphabet soup of letters denoting engine, wing design and model sub-type. This elegant wheel-spatted three-seater photographed at the Experimental Aircraft Association's Sun 'n Fun fly-in at Lakeland, Florida is one of the 1931/33 BF/CF series, the precise engine designator prefix depending on whether it has a 170 hp Jacobs or 165/210 hp Continental powerplant. It's a brave man who'd hazard a guess

Yankee Doodle

The classic Stearman biplane was one of the few things the US Army and US Navy ever agreed upon. Both services ordered it in the mid-1930s and used it as a primary trainer throughout the Second World War. First flown in December 1933, the Stearman paradoxically had no more than a tenuous connection with the man whose name it bears. Lloyd Stearman had left the Wichita-based company which he founded two years before the designers Harold Zipp and Jack Clark revealed the Model 70 from which this aeroplane evolved, and the 'Stearman' was a product of Boeing's Stearman Division. A total of 10,346 were built as Lycoming-engined PT-13 and Continental-powered PT-17 Kaydets for the Army and N2Ss for the Navy, whose aircraft were known as *Yellow Perils* because of their bright colour schemes designed to warn other aviators that they were being flown by trainee pilots. Much bigger, stronger and with roomier cockpits than its British counterpart the Tiger Moth, the Stearman was widely used in peacetime for training among smaller air forces, formed the backbone of the crop-dusting industry in the United States, and continues to enjoy popularity as an airshow mount (often with 450 hp Pratt & Whitney Wasp radials replacing the original 220-280 hp powerplants) and as a collectable 'warbird'. This one, photographed at Sun 'n Fun, is finished in the True Blue and Chrome Yellow colours of USAAC Kaydets

These pages Sharing primary training duties with the Stearman biplane was the Fairchild PT-19, developed from the commercial Model M-62. The most numerous variant, seen here taxiing at Sun 'n Fun, was the 200 hp Ranger L-440-3-engined PT-19A, 3703 of which were built by Fairchild, Aeronca and the St Louis company. The later model PT-23, seen aloft from its base at Cosford, England, where it is part of Bob Mitchell's PT Flight airshow circus, was powered by a 220 hp Continental R-670 radial engine. A total of 1126 PT-23 primary trainers and PT-23A blind-flying trainers was built by Fairchild, Howard Aircraft Corporation and Fleet in Canada. Production ended with 670 Ranger-powered PT-26s which were supplied to the Royal Canadian Air Force as Cornell Mk Is and 1057 PT-26A/Bs for the USAAC. Unlike those illustrated here, all Cornells and PT-26 variants had fully-enclosed cockpits with long sliding canopies

Right and overleaf Having learned the rudiments of airmanship on Stearmans and Fairchilds, the next step up the training ladder brought cadet pilots into contact with this machine, officially known as the Vultee Valiant, but popularly (?) dubbed Vultee Vibrator because of the all-over massage job its 450 hp radial engine gave occupants. The most extensively produced US wartime basic trainer, the Valiant was built in two main versions. The BT-13A/B, first ordered in 1939, was powered by a 450 hp Pratt & Whitney R-985-25 Wasp Junior radial, production totalling 7832. Shortage of Wasp engines resulted in the Wright R-975-11-engined BT-15, of which 1693 were built. Two thousand USAAC BT-13A/Bs were transferred to the US Navy as SNV-1/2s. This aircraft is one of only three examples of the now rare Wright-powered BT-15 known to be flying, and is another of Englishman Bob Mitchell's PT Flight 'cradles of heroes' collection. Despite the large numbers of 'Vibrators' built, few survive in airworthy condition, and many that have were converted into replica Japanese Kate and Val torpedo bombers for such movies as *Tora! Tora! Tora!*

Below Instructor's eye view of the 'Vibrator'. Triangular structure between the cockpits is a roll-over pylon designed to prevent the canopy collapsing and trapping or crushing the occupants in the event of a (not uncommon) nose-over on landing

Vintage RAF

Roy Chadwick, later to create the Lancaster bomber, designed the Avro 621 Tutor in 1929 as a successor in Royal Air Force service to the venerable Avro 504K. Powered by a 240 hp Armstrong-Siddeley Lynx IVC seven-cylinder radial, the Tutor was a large, comfortable and well-equipped aeroplane for its role as a trainer, having spacious cockpits with adjustable seats, mainwheel brakes, a tailwheel rather than the then more common skid, and a variable incidence tailplane for pitch trimming, and was easier to fly than many of its contemporaries, perhaps even a touch too docile to make a really great training aeroplane. From 1933–36 six sunburst-striped Tutors made up the Central Flying School's formation aerobatic team — a distant and unnamed forerunner of today's Red Arrows — while more mundanely the aircraft served with the RAF College, with Nos 3, 5 and 11 Flying Training Schools at RAF Grantham, RAF Sealand and RAF Wittering, and with the Oxford and Cambridge University Air Squadrons. In addition to the RAF, Tutor variants also served with the Danish Navy, and the air forces of Brazil, Egypt, Greece and South Africa and in small numbers with civilian operators

Above The Shuttleworth Collection's K3215, resplendent in pre-war Trainer Yellow paint with polished cowling, is the sole survivor of 855 Tutors built by A V Roe & Co Ltd and a further 60 licence-built in South Africa and Denmark. Formerly with the RAF College at Cranwell — whose crest it wears on its fin — and with the RAF Central Flying School, it was the last Tutor in RAF service when struck off charge in December 1946

Below The traditional 'Armstrong' method of hand-propping aeroplanes was fine when engines were small and low powered, but as the number of cylinders, power output and propeller size increased, starting became a problem. Enter B C Hucks, one of the most famous British pioneer aviators. He took the chassis of a Model T Ford and mounted on it a starting mechanism whose chain-and-sprocket driven shaft has a spring-loaded cross-head which engages a claw or 'dog' on the propeller boss. The car's engine drive is selectable to propel the Model T normally or to operate the shaft, as seen here on the Shuttleworth Collection's uniquely operational Hucks Starter cranking up the Tutor's Lynx engine

These pages Like the Tutor, the 1928 Hawker Tomtit was also designed as an Avro 504N replacement, and introduced a number of innovations previously unseen on an elementary trainer, including automatic slots on its upper wings, a full blind flying panel with flight-operable blind-flying hood for the rear cockpit, and heavily-staggered wings making rapid exit by parachute easy from either cockpit. The engine was a 150 hp Armstrong-Siddeley Mongoose IIIC five-cylinder radial. Despite its delightful handling qualities the RAF ordered only 25 Tomtits, which served with No 3 Flying Training School at RAF Grantham and with the Central Flying School at RAF Wittering, while one was attached to No 24 Sqn on communications duties at RAF Northolt near London, where it was regularly flown by the then Prince of Wales. Withdrawn from RAF service in 1935, a number of Tomtits were sold on the civilian market, including the Shuttleworth Collection's K1786/G-AFTA, the last production aircraft and sole survivor which was owned post-war by Hawker test pilot and one-time world airspeed record holder Squadron Leader Neville Duke

These pages and overleaf Throughout the 1930s Hawker biplanes formed the backbone of Royal Air Force fighter and bomber strength, from the Fury single-seat and Demon two-seat fighters through numerous variants of the ubiquitous Hart filling almost every conceivable role from trainer, target tug and army co-operation aircraft to light day bomber. The Hind seen here replaced the Hart in 1935 as part of the RAF's pre-war expansion scheme and differed from its predecessor in having a supercharged Rolls-Royce Kestrel V V-12 engine which put out 640 hp – 115 hp more than the Hart's Kestrel IB – a cut-away rear cockpit to provide a better field of fire for the gunner's flexible-mount Lewis gun, an improved exhaust system, and a tailwheel instead of a skid.

The Shuttleworth Collection's Hind was one of eight supplied new to the Royal Afghan Air Force in 1938, ten surplus RAF machines following two years later. Not retired until 1956, it lay at Bagram, north of Kabul, until 1970 when it was presented to the Collection and brought back to England in an epic 6000-mile overland journey, and is seen here as originally restored in the Afghan colours in which it made its first flight for a quarter of a century on 17 August 1981.

Now bearing the serial number K5414 and the crest and Roman-numeral marking of No 15 Sqn Royal Air Force, which operated Hinds from RAF Abingdon near Oxford but now flies Tornados, the Shuttleworth machine epitomises the golden (or rather the silver and polished aluminium) era of RAF aviation. Appropriately for this last RAF biplane light bomber, an added touch of realism has been added with bomb racks and convincing glassfibre 120 lb Mk 1 general purpose high explosive bombs

Just as the Hind saw out the biplane era among RAF bomber squadrons, so was the Gloster Gladiator its last biplane fighter, and, paradoxically, its first to have a fully-enclosed cockpit. Other Gladiator novelties were its flaps (on all four wings) and four Browning 0.303 machine guns – two mounted either side of the forward fuselage, another pair in blisters beneath the lower wings – which doubled the firepower of its predecessors. Despite the 840 hp produced by its Bristol Mercury IX nine-cylinder radial, the Gladiator suffered the inevitable drag of its fixed-undercarriage bestrutted biplane configuration, and with a top speed of 253 mph depended on manoeuvrability for the success of legendary overseas actions fought during the Second World War in the Arctic and in the defence of Malta. On the home front the Gladiator had been largely replaced by the Spitfire and Hurricane by the outbreak of war, but during the Battle of Britain Gladiators of No 247 Sqn based at Roborough, Devon, were charged with defence of the Royal Naval dockyards at Plymouth, and the Shuttleworth Collection's unique airworthy machine was repainted in 247's camouflage colours for the 50th Anniversary celebrations in 1990

Above *Maggie, Maggie, Maggie!* Derived from the pre-war Hawk light aircraft, the more robust Miles M.14A Magister was the RAF's first monoplane trainer and the first to have flaps. Of all-wood construction with a 130 hp D.H. Gipsy Major I four-cylinder engine, the Magister was intended to introduce student pilots to the handling characteristics of the new monoplane fighters, Spitfire and Hurricane. With its abrupt stall and need for positive and precise spin recovery action (not to mention an odd quirk of aerodynamics whereby inadvertent sideslip would cause the fin and rudder to blanket airflow over the tailplane and elevator causing a pitch-down and occasionally fatal terminal dive), the Magister was less well-suited to the role of primary trainer than its biplane counterpart the Tiger Moth. Deliveries began in September 1937, a total of 1242 Maggies eventually joining the RAF, in which they served 16 Elementary Flying Training Schools. The Shuttleworth Collection's wartime-camouflaged P6382/G -AJDR is one of only two still airworthy . . .

Below and overleaf . . . the other is Adrian Brook's meticulously restored V1075/G-AKPF in glorious pre-war RAF trainer livery and wearing the beauty-enhancing but prone-to-clogging undercarriage 'trousers' and wheel spats which were quickly dispensed with in wartime. Why have so few Magisters survived? Because, on 18 September 1957 – a day of infamy if ever there was one for light aircraft owners – the British Airworthiness Requirements Board issued a directive that all ageing wood-skinned aircraft had to be dismantled and opened up for inspection for potentially catastrophic glue failure and all suspect timber and glued joints made good. The cost of such total rebuilds far exceeded the values of most pre-war and wartime-surplus airframes, and large numbers of now rare aeroplanes were simply broken up or burned. G-AKPF once part of a large RAF Elementary Flying Training School fleet based at

Burnaston, near Derby (now, lamentably, a Toyota car factory), had been sold as surplus for £50 in 1947 and raced by Ron Paine. While on the strength of Air Schools, again at Burnaston, it crashed after a full-power spin at low-level, and underwent a major rebuild which fortunately met the requirements of the draconian ARB directive and saved it from the bonfire. Finally retired in 1962, it returned to the air 28 years and many thousands of dedicated man-hours later, owner Brook's efforts rewarded when the magnificent Maggie won the Best Vintage Aircraft and Concours d'Elegance trophies at the Popular Flying Association's annual rally in 1991

Below V1075/G-AKPF's cockpits are totally authentic, right down to its enormous P8 compasses and turn & slip indicators, vertical glass tube pitch attitude indicators, Phillips & Powis Aircraft Ltd manufacturer's plates and even a contemporary 1940 navigation chart! Note the three-piece framed windscreen for the front cockpit incorporating a roll-over arch, and the simple but more effective curved Perspex screen for the student in the rear

These pages First appearing as the D.H.89 Dragon Six six-passenger airliner in
1934, the Dragon Rapide soon became a mainstay of short-haul air carriers in
pre-war Britain and played a major part in opening internal air routes, notably
in Scotland. In wartime the military Dominie fulfilled numerous roles,
particularly as a navigator/radio operator trainer and liaison/communications
aircraft. A total of 727 Dragon Rapides and Dominies were built by de
Havilland and by the Brush Coachworks at Loughborough in Leicestershire,
where most wartime production took place while D.H.'s Hatfield plant
concentrated on Mosquitoes. For a decade or more after war's end Dragon
Rapides and civilianised Dominies again swelled the fleets of what would now
be called 'third level' or 'commuter' airlines, and serviced short routes for some
major carriers, including British European Airways, which employed them on its
Scottish Highlands and Islands services. Z7260/G-AHGD *Women of the Empire*
is a wartime Dominie, finished as one of two ambulance aircraft subscribed for
by the Silver Thimble Fund and handed over to the RAF at Hendon on 21 May
1941 by Lady Maud Carnegie. Owned for many years by The Honourable
Michael Astor and loaned to the Shuttleworth Collection's de Havilland Flying
Centre, it was sold at auction to a private collector in 1991 and was
subsequently destroyed in a tragic fatal crash while taking part in an air display
in Essex

Dragon Rapides also found favour as luxury private transports and executive aircraft. Among the most luxurious was G-ACTT, owned by His Royal Highness Prince Edward, the Prince of Wales in 1935, and his similarly plush G-ADDD which became the first aircraft operated by the King's Flight of the Royal Air Force when it was formed on 21 July 1936. G-ACZE was built in 1934 as an executive aircraft for the Anglo-Persian Oil Company. Half a century later master craftsman and arch de Havilland enthusiast Ron Souch began restoration of its derelict airframe, completing the aircraft in the striking red and blue Brigade of Guards livery worn by the 'royal' Rapides (note the Prince of Wales's crest on its fin), with interior appointments to match. A gentleman's carriage fit for a king indeed, and greatly enjoyed by owner Brian Woodward, who maintains an enviable collection of de Havilland light aircraft at his country manor in Dorset

Above Like Miles Magisters, Percival Proctors were put to the torch by the score following the 'glue scare' of 1957, and are now very rare. Developed from the pre-war Gull and Vega Gull, three-seat Proctor Is, IIs and IIIs and four-seat Proctor IVs served the RAF as communications aircraft and wireless operator trainers throughout the war years, some remaining in service until 1955. This one is a Proctor IV, with 210 hp D.H. Gipsy Queen II engine

The British called it the Harvard, the US Army Air Corps knew it as the Texan, while to trainee pilots in the US Navy it was an SNJ. Call it what you will the North American AT-6 was one of the most successful advanced training aeroplanes of all times. Developed specifically for a British Air Ministry requirement for just 200 aircraft, the first Harvard made its maiden flight on 28 September 1938. Within a year demand from Britain, Canada, the United States and elsewhere was being met from two North American factories at Inglewood, California and Dallas Texas, and from the Canadian Norduyn Aviation plant. By 1942 pilots from 23 nations were learning to fly and fight in the aircraft. Production or remanufacture of T-6/Harvard variants continued into the early 1950s. A total of 15,495 of all models was built. They served with the air arms of more than 40 countries, training over 131,500 aircrew in the British Commonwealth Air Training Plan alone during the Second World War. A few Harvards continue to train military pilots with smaller air forces around the world, but now the aeroplane has deservedly become a treasured collector's item. G-AZSC, seen here being displayed in characteristically spirited fashion by the late Neil Williams with fellow British Aerobatic Team member James Black 'along for the ride', now wears Japanese markings to masquerade as a Mitsubishi Zero fighter in the Harvard Formation Team's Pacific War airshow 'set-piece', flown by owner, pop star and warbird enthusiast Gary 'Banzai!' Numan